WHAT WOULD LOVE SAY TODAY?

Copyright © 2022 by Lavinia Lord

All rights reserved. No part of this book may be reproduced in any manner whatsoever without written permission except in the case of brief quotations embodied in critical articles and reviews.

First Printing, 2022
by Off-Trail Publishing
PO Box 656
Harpers Ferry, WV 25425
USA

Cover photo: Elizabeth Sealey

ISBN 978-0-578-92089-4

WHAT WOULD LOVE SAY TODAY?

*100 poems in
100 days
Volume I*

LAVINIA LORD

Off-Trail Publishing

Dedication

Contents

Gratitude — xiv

PROLOGUE — 1

TO: LOVE #1 — 8

FROM: LOVE #1 — 10

FROM: LOVE #2 — 12

TO: LOVE #2 — 14

FROM: LOVE #3 — 16

TO: LOVE #3 — 18

FROM: LOVE #4 — 20

FROM: LOVE #5 — 22

TO: LOVE #4 — 24

FROM: LOVE #6 — 26

FROM: LOVE #7	27
FROM: LOVE #8	29
FROM: LOVE #9	30
FROM: LOVE #10	32
FROM: LOVE #11	34
FROM: LOVE #12	35
FROM: LOVE #13	37
FROM: LOVE #14	39
FROM: LOVE #15	41
FROM: LOVE #16	43
FROM: LOVE #17	45
FROM: LOVE #18	47
FROM: LOVE #19	49
FROM: LOVE #20	51
FROM: LOVE #21	53
FROM: LOVE #22	55
FROM: LOVE #23	58
FROM: LOVE #24	60

FROM: LOVE #25	62
FROM: LOVE #26	64
FROM: LOVE #27	67
FROM: LOVE #28	69
FROM: LOVE #29	71
FROM: LOVE #30	73
FROM: LOVE #31	75
FROM: LOVE #32	77
FROM: LOVE #33	79
FROM: LOVE #34	81
FROM: LOVE #35	83
FROM: LOVE #36	86
FROM: LOVE #37	88
FROM: LOVE #38	90
FROM: LOVE #39	92
FROM: LOVE #40	94
FROM: LOVE #41	96
FROM: LOVE #42	99

FROM: LOVE #43	101
FROM: LOVE #44	104
FROM: LOVE #45	106
FROM: LOVE #46	108
FROM: LOVE #47	110
FROM: LOVE #48	112
FROM: LOVE #49	114
FROM: LOVE #50	116
FROM: LOVE #51	118
FROM: LOVE #52	121
FROM: LOVE #53	124
FROM: LOVE #54	126
FROM: LOVE #55	128
FROM: LOVE #56	130
FROM: LOVE #57	132
FROM: LOVE #58	135
FROM: LOVE #59	137
FROM: LOVE #60	139

FROM: LOVE #61	141
FROM: LOVE #62	143
FROM: LOVE #63	145
FROM: LOVE #64	147
FROM: LOVE #65	149
FROM: LOVE #66	151
FROM: LOVE #67	153
FROM: LOVE #68	155
FROM: LOVE #69	157
FROM: LOVE #70	159
FROM: LOVE #71	161
FROM: LOVE #72	163
FROM: LOVE #73	165
FROM: LOVE #74	167
FROM: LOVE #75	169
FROM: LOVE #76	171
FROM: LOVE #77	173
FROM: LOVE #78	175

FROM: LOVE #79	177
FROM: LOVE #80	179
FROM: LOVE #81	181
FROM: LOVE #82	183
FROM: LOVE #83	184
FROM: LOVE #84	186
FROM: LOVE #85	188
FROM: LOVE #86	189
FROM: LOVE #87	191
FROM: LOVE #88	194
FROM: LOVE #89	196
FROM: LOVE #90	198
FROM: LOVE #91	200
FROM: LOVE #92	203
FROM: LOVE #93	206
FROM: LOVE #94	208
FROM: LOVE #95	211
FROM: LOVE #96	213

Contents ~ xiii

FROM: LOVE #97	215
FROM: LOVE #98	217
FROM: LOVE #99	219
FROM: LOVE #100	222
EPILOGUE	224
BIBLIOGRAPHY	229

Gratitude

To my mum, Joanie, for your example of innocent curiosity that opens the doors to creativity in every moment and brings playful delight in the discovery of what unfolds. This approach lay the groundwork for this experiment.

To my papa, Ernest, for your tenacity and sheer determination that I, in turn, found within myself to move through dense territory to reach higher ground.

To my extended family for your interest and engagement in language and words that I once found intimidating, but now am starting to find surprisingly enjoyable and satisfying.

To Lara, Ross, Kineta, Titi, and Bronwyn, thank you for seeing me all these years, when I couldn't see myself, and for the inspiration your bring to me with your resplendent presence on this Earth.

To the Creative Alchemists, Jillian, Phyllis, Sarah, Laurie and Jeanette, for our explorations of the creative process, expression, and beauty. Your own creativity has kept mine alive, and I am deeply grateful for your reliable, compassionate and humorous company along the way.

To Agathe and Maria Grazia, your contributions to this experience were vast and deep. We just keep rolling, don't we!

To Allie, for each of our rich, colorful, emergent conversations that brings us closer to our wild essence, and invites in fresh new ways to lead others to the voice of their hearts. Thank you for your faith that I may have something to offer with these poems.

Merci pour les bonnes rigolades, chère Muriel. Que ferait-on sans le pouvoir du rire et sans la compagnie des fleurs qui nous entourent.

To Captain Pat and his Morgan 38, for the many inspiring sails together. Several of these poems were written aboard the majestic Sarah Effie in the Chesapeake Bay. Thank you for your endless hospitality.

Thank you, Kim and Miss Jenny, for showing me good new friends are possible, even as a result of parallel experiences. It has been so much fun to grow along side you. That's cool.

And of course, to David Whyte for his willingness to engage so beautifully with life and invite others gracefully to open a little more to the transparent magnificence of our experience here together. Your conversational approach really opened a world and way that allowed me to embody and include myself into my own life. Thank you ever so deeply.

I am grateful to this precious planet we live on and all the elements, the plants, trees, flowers and food that continue to flourish despite the challenges, and to the animals who also teach us to stay pure. Your presence enhanced this experiment in transcendent and humbling ways. Our experience here wouldn't exist without you.

Finally, I thank Love itself, for playing in this experiment with me and for showing up with me day after day. Your devotion was astonishing, your expression always on point, your wisdom consistently grounding, and your spontaneity continually refreshing. Getting to know you has been an unexpected and extraordinary pleasure.

I LOVE YOU ALL

PROLOGUE

This book came to life as an experiment, from a reality of what Love is not. It all started with a blow-up conversation, well, several, actually. And a lingering question around, "what is it that escalates painful interactions?" In the middle of it all, at the core of the escalation, I found fear. Fear brought denial and lies. Fear brought blame and disconnection. Fear brought more fear and pain, doubt and defensiveness. Resentment and exclusion.

In the middle of a significant personal and professional transformation, it became clear that for the work I was meant to do in this life, I absolutely needed to express myself through pure Love, without a trace of fear. I already knew expressing through fear was clearly ineffective. Even if I was afraid, I was going to have to learn to express it through Love. But what did that even mean? No idea. I just knew I had to learn it.

Simultaneously, I was reading *The Voice of Knowledge*, by Don Miguel Ruiz, who caught my attention with his Toltec perspective of love.

> *How can you believe someone who says, "I love you," and then treats you with disrespect and emotional violence? How can someone say, "I love you," when that person wants to control your life, to tell you what you have to do, what you have to believe? How can someone claim to love you, and then give you emotional garbage, jealousy, envy?*
>
> *How can we tell someone, "I love you," and then send all our opinions against the person we love to try to make that person suffer? I have to tell you what is wrong with you, because "I love you." I have to judge you, find you guilty, and punish you, because "I love you." I have to make you wrong all the time, and make you feel like you are good for nothing, because "I love you." And because you love me, you have to put up with my anger, my jealousy, with all my stupidity.*

> *Do you think this is love? This is not love. This is nothing but selfishness and we call it love. (Ruiz, 174-175)*

Wow. That woke me right up. It further opened the intrigue… "if that wasn't love, what *was* love?"

Meanwhile, in a poetry series I had started a few weeks prior, David Whyte, the brave and brilliant Anglo-Irish poet, had just invited us to explore unresolved grief, by connecting to the feeling and writing directly from there; to see what grief had to say through a conversation (2020). Other than one or two poems here and there, I had never written poetry, so, green behind the ears, I tried it out wholeheartedly. To my surprise, the elements of a long-buried heartbreak emerged into a poem that wrote itself and left me lighter, wiser, and feeling more whole. The experience was incredibly liberating; the voice that spoke came from such a deep truth I didn't realize was inside.

It's important to presence, that the context of all of this unfolding coincided with the time of George Floyd's murder, in the wake of so many others, horrifically kneeled on by a police officer until he could no longer breathe. It was a clear declaration of systemic fear, by this white man in a position of authority, exemplified through this addition to long-standing systemic racism. Covid 19 was just starting to gain momentum, contributing its own chaos, and affecting the breathing systems of thousands of people around the world. We were expected to stay home. These synchronistic threads reconnected me to the preciousness of breathing - the essence of life itself.

Back to the drawing board of our collective society, the emerging practices of healing collective trauma and heart-centered living were paralleling and counteracting our unhealthy paths. Other inspiration came from John Lewis's memoir, *Walking with the Wind (1998)*, Bryan Stevenson's exceptional work standing for integrity in the US justice system, and the inspirational peace-building work of the MOSAIC Project in the Bay Area, led by Lara Mendel and Brian Lowe. And complementary to the social justice, was the work of Doctor Ramani, Dr Les Carter, and Lisa A. Romano focusing on surviving narcissism.

While I may not mention these directly in the poetry, they brought grounding and sanity, as they fused with my explorations. What if instead of having a system of centralized fear we could have a decentralized system of Love? What if everyone had their own direct access to Love? What would a whole system of Love be like?

I want to be clear that this experiment was not about "self-love." For those of us who have self-destruction or self-loathing in our background, or for anyone who feels unlovable, telling us to "Love yourself" or say, "I am Love" is like asking someone to light a fire underwater. The big difference is: I don't have to feel lovable in order to *access* Love.

This experiment was to connect to the *essence* of love in and of itself, through conversation, so I could better understand how it worked, how it moved, how it spoke, what it felt like, and hear it through my own "love voice." I am an experiential educator by profession, and it's my go-to for learning as well. So, I used my own laboratory: my own body, my own reactions, my own story with all the feelings to engage in the process. I had to learn to be truly and transparently honest with myself to do it. Otherwise, I couldn't bring Love into the world with authenticity.

What would it sound like? Would I be able to recognize it? Would I be worthy of this conversation? Where would my voice be in all this? I had very rarely heard my own true voice. I needed to design a Love Trip immersion for myself, so, since we were on lockdown, I went inward.

I had recently tapped into what I called the "inside scoop" of my feelings and needs - I was the only one who had direct access to what I felt and what I needed, yet I was deeply disconnected. I wondered, "if I could have a conversation with Grief, would Love be available to me too? Could Love show me (the subject of the experiment) how to honor, acknowledge, and express my feelings and needs?" This was not something I had done. So, in David Whyte conversational style, I committed to open to Love, by writing myself a poem from Love, every day for 100 days.

Approaching it like I was leading an expedition into the wilderness, I set off on a discovery of Love in my own inner landscape. Every day I would sit in stillness, and ask myself, "What would Love say to me today?" I would listen inside, with genuine curiosity and innocence, as if getting to know a new friend, and write what came through.

In the spirit of conversation, you'll notice that in the beginning I wrote back to Love. It soon came clear, however, that this would require way more energy than I would be able to sustain for 100 days. Besides, I realized that part of what I needed to learn in this process was how to *receive* love, and listen to what it had to say.

I had no intention of publishing these poems. From my conditioning, I experienced that no one could relate to me, and everything I felt was wrong. But I shared some poems with others, and they found resonance, like an echo of their own experiences, or of the work they were doing with their clients. So here they are, in hopes that you may find some solace, or inspiration for your own experiment to discover Love for yourself, which is ultimately my wish for everyone.

At the end of the book, I explain a little more about my experience through the process, and the impact of this experiment, but for now, I will just invite you in...

PS – "Chispita" is an endearing nickname from a friend, that means "Little Spark" in Spanish, because I can be quick to ignite.

TO: LOVE #1

Saturday, 30 May 2020

The softness that fills my body
is like an echo of the
fluffy clouds
moving gently overhead
at a pace where I want to
notice even the slightest change
because each form it
takes has its own shape,
its own original
vibration of visual joy.
It's a new river of
Sensations that
have a power I am
just beginning to access;
just beginning to understand

that I too can offer them
a home to flow in,
a haven of safety.
I feel the freshness of
green lettuce in my mouth
with all its curly leaves
ready to be savored,
ready to nourish all the cells in my
Being.
And in the background,
the melodies of Spring
bouncing off the
flowers.
What a pleasure it is to mee you, LOVE.
I'm opening to your shape-shifting
Magic because I can see what a
delightful journey it will be
if I play the game
in seeing how many places
I can find you.

FROM: LOVE #1

Saturday, 30 May 2020

Dear precious child of many names,
you have been so brave.
You have been able to
come through the darkest of darks
and still have a phenomenal
determination to stay
true to your core,
even when you didn't know how,
even when you couldn't tell who you could trust.
That's how you can see in the dark now.
That's how you can hear through silence.
You have the resourcefulness
of a scavenger,
the tenacity of a
dung beetle,

the endurance of
a penguin,
the curiosity of a cat.
And what you may not
have had a chance to
realize yet,
is that you also have the elegance of
a swan
the cleverness and playfulness of a sea otter,
the glow of a firefly,
the courage of a honey badger.
Welcome Home, dear one.
You can rest here.
Welcome Home.
I am here with you now.
I will be with you,
always.

FROM: LOVE #2

Sunday, 31 May 2020

I love that you use everything
to its maximum capacity.
You are a beauty
of nature in that vein.
I wonder if you can hear
me when I say,
You are precious.
I wonder if you can feel
the power that courses
through your voice
that you have
held back
on may occasion.
Go ahead and practice.
You will always have

those who love you,
like me.

TO: LOVE #2

Monday, 1 June 2020

I found you this morning
as the grass beneath my bare feet.
I found you in a bowl of vanilla
almond yogurt, topped
with amber maple syrup.
I found you weaving through
the rich conversations
of growth and expansion.
You came as a check in the mail
with a friendly note from Eddie.
I smell you in the eucalyptus
incense atop
a tea-light candle,
and I hear you in the
music emanating

from the bright red speakers
I bought myself last fall,
that's mixing with the
chortling of the birds
at the end of a beautiful day.
Hooray, I say!
You're here!
Come again tomorrow.
I'll be here too.

FROM: LOVE #3

Monday, 1 June 2020

I'm here.
I know.
I know what you've been through.
I know you've been scared.
I trust you can learn,
Your skill to discern
The Yes from the No,
The ally from the foe.
There will come a time for
your song to be sung
to the sun and the sky above,
to the shooting starts of bright Love.
But your heart has been wrung,
and it's time to pause.
Pause in the sacred space.

Fill it with all your grace.
Allow yourself to listen for your pace,
That you may be free
Free of what you have held
You've been through the grief,
The loss and the pain
Release it
Release it to the wind
Let it go off with the train
Let it ALL GO
I feel the tingles in your body
That speak to the relief
Relief of the heavy load.
Lightness is your new mode.
Let us sit here together
Allowing the weather
To pass...

How about a hot shower?

TO: LOVE #3

Tuesday, 2 June 2020

In the morning
I felt you in the hot tears
running down my face.
You gave me a pillow
and wrapped me in a blanket
to keep me warm
because you know that
cold is what happens to my body
when it's frozen in fright.
The heavy drums played
a rhythm that encouraged
my heartbeat to stay steady.
Later, I went to the woods
to breathe...
I heard you in the susurration

of the forest leaves
in the gentle breeze.
I felt you in the presence
of the white butterfly
pausing its fluttery flight
on a violet leaf right next to me,
the black ant crawling its way
around my toes.
I smelled you in the sweet waft
of honeysuckle rising
from the cliffs below.
You bring life to all of my sensations, Love.
You give so freely.
What can I give to you?

FROM: LOVE #4

Tuesday, 2 June 2020

Your curiosity warms my heart,
with innocence it does impart
A place for my becoming.

In seeking me as if a treasure
Your gift of love gives such great pleasure
Letting all assumptions go
Opens doors to let me show
True Love without a measure

Then were those who posed as me
They took you away
They brought you despair
Pretending to care
or not knowing where

they were going themselves
leaving their hearts
upon the shelves.

I thought you were gone
You went in so deep
You had the obedience
of a blind sheep.

But that's not the essence
of your core.
The lion inside
has courage galore,
and she is the one
awakening now.
She is the one
who's ready for more.

But let's go easy
Let's go slow
Just to Be with you today
Brings me home to my Dear Lei

FROM: LOVE #5

Wednesday, 3 June 2020

(Hi) I would like to start this day
with a love note to Dear Lei.
I'm holding you with Love so tender
In a way that you can render
The fullness true of who you are,
The fragile parts that've come so far.
It's okay that you are scared,
Wondering who really cared,
Acknowledging they did their best
With their own pain and all the rest.
But let us come back to your heart
The most important loving part
That now stands on solid ground
Feeling finally that you've found
Your own voice in its pure essence.

Your heart is bright like phosphorescence
Lighting up with all the waves.
I know that you truly care.
How about we start from there?
I love you, Dear Lavinia
I love you (v)
I love you (v)
I love you (v)

TO: LOVE #4

Wednesday, 3 June 2020

I have been looking for you
in all the wrong places,
and I am terrified
to open to you,
because I've been
mis-taken so many times before
that my trust in my
own judgment
has eroded.
So, please be gentle with me.
I'm willing to try again,
as long as you can
understand that my
resistance comes from a
fear of being wrong

again, then making
everything worse.
Please be gentle with me.
I need some spaciousness
to un-learn my warped
impression of who
and what you are.

FROM: LOVE #6

Thursday, 4 June 2020

The way you move through
Every day
Never ceases to
Amaze me. Your
Commitment
Is
Obvious and
Undeniable
Success is bound to follow

FROM: LOVE #7

Friday, 5 June 2020

I was the one who
called you outside
in the garden this afternoon
to celebrate with the Universe today.
As the rain pattered
upon your up-turned face,
and washed over your whole
body, its wet cleansing
seeping through
your clothes to touch your skin
with the soothing rhythm
of the raindrops,
I was the dark grey slab of limestone
you stood on
that held the heat

of the morning sun
keeping your feet warm
and reminding
you that
I am here.

FROM: LOVE #8

Saturday, 6 June 2020

3 Haikus

Stepping through the veil
Going deep into yearning
Celebrate full moon

Getting to the core
On your way to Everything
Discover what's next

Know that I love you
I will be with you always
We are a good team

FROM: LOVE #9

Sunday, 7 June 2020

Gentle
Today I offer
Gentle Love
to ease your nerves
and bless your heart,
to please and serve
and help you start
afresh,
aware,
aligned
with your essence.
You have a beauty
deep inside.
I am a cutie
and provide

the kind of Love
that only
you will know
is right for you.
And today,
it's Gentle Love
Gentle
Gentle
Gentle

FROM: LOVE #10

Monday, 8 June 2020

Dear lovely Lei
    Lavinia
    Vinie
    Firelily
Here are some of
the strengths I see
in you...
    Navigation
    Utilization
    Patience
    Tenacity
    Playfulness
    Analysis
    Math/proportional calculation
    Design

They can go with you
anywhere.
Just like me –
I will go with you
anywhere.

FROM: LOVE #11

Tuesday, 9 June 2020

My Love for you
is Big and Bold
it's Bright and Sassy
it's Light
    and Classy
It holds the energy of a rainbow
    doubled over,
The focus of a bumblebee
    on a white Dutch clover
The devotion that offers
an eternity
without question
of a reliable source
of nectar.

FROM: LOVE #12

Wednesday, 10 June 2020

Would you believe
I love you
even if you're white?
Would you believe
I love
the way you fight?
Would you believe
that I love you
even if you struggle
to open for support?
even when you
don't know
what to do
or who to trust
or how to listen

to yourself
amongst all
the voices?
I love that you
keep trying
you keep getting
back up
back into the
ring.
And whether you
believe it or not,
even if...
no matter what,
I'll be in your corner
and I will sing:
I love you, Lavinia !
I love you, Vinie !!
I love youuu !!!

FROM: LOVE #13

Thursday, 11 June 2020

Oh honey,
you're scared.
You're scared
you'll get thrown back,
back to before.
You keep discovering
more sorrows,
more losses.
But they aren't the bosses.
>We are.
>You and I.

We get to write the guest list.
We get to make the pie.
We get to say, "I love you"
and know the reasons why.

Breathe.
Just breathe.
Breathe in the love
    I have for you
Breathe in the care
    that's just and true.
Breathe in the knowing
deep in your heart
that you hold truth
and wisdom smart.
Don't give up now
you've come so far.
I'm holding your hand,
seeing your shooting star.

FROM: LOVE #14

Friday, 12 June 2020

Good for you
for staying the course.
As the unfolding
of this new chapter
presents a
different landscape,
your brilliance
in moving in the
dark, without being able
to see where
you're going
can only enhance
your other
senses,
can only serve

to open doors you
do not know are
there.

FROM: LOVE #15

Saturday, 13 June 2020

Feel the Love in the bench gently swinging
In the kora the fingers are singing

Drink it in, with the espresso, so hot
Dream it big with the Parks pass you bought

Flashed, in the smile from your friend at the store
Felt, through the warmth in the wood of the floor

This love is yours, for you to partake
Leaving joy in its fabulous wake

I'm going slow. Lemme know when you're
ready
for more of the flow, and none of the Betty

We're good to go now
you can rest and know how

I'll be everywhere, if you look
in the music, or in a book

in the light, at the end of the day
in the song of the birds at play

We'll keep exploring, you and me
May this vibrant love let you go free.

FROM: LOVE #16

Sunday, 14 June 2020

May you continue
to discover the "Yes's"
that fill your heart
with the reverberation
that echoes
through to your
soul's deepest
recognition of its
own awakening.
May you continue
to find your wisdom
in the depths of
your being
in its purity
and brilliant essence

of humility and
aspiration.
And may your heart's
conviction
move you in tune
with the alignment
you seek to
integrate with
the music and rhythm
of your highest life.

    With blessings,
             LOVE

FROM: LOVE #17

Monday, 15 June 2020

Today is a Monday of Alchemy
where doors previously shut to you
open with welcoming fanfare
and in the name of Love,
I declare "en directo"...
You get to need what you need
You get to say yes or no
You are the $15 sheet of paper
    made of high-quality materials
    highly cared for, created with
    thoughtful brilliance and effort
You get to slow down
You get to let yourself explore
You get to decide what to do
You get to choose

You get to define what comfort means
You get to connect to your power
You get to be grounded and centered
You get to access support
You get to write a "whatever" poem
   at midnight
You get to receive Love
You get to "Press on the upward way"
You get to plant your feet on higher ground
You get to have friends
You get to laugh
You get to rest
You get to live your life
   as part of the whole
You get your truth back
You are free

*Inspired in part by the Creative Alchemists meeting this day (and Jillian Shillig's $15 sheet of paper idea), and the 2019 film *Just Mercy*, based on Bryan Stevenson's book, *Just Mercy: A Story of Justice and Redemption*. New York: Spiegel & Grau, 2014

FROM: LOVE #18

Tuesday, 16 June 2020

If only you knew
How rich your
imagination really is,
how your creative Love,
and expression of it,
shine rainbows through storms.
I wonder how I can
help you drop your guard
enough to surrender
to what is truly
inside.
For in that knowing
you will be even more
supported because
your you-ness in its simplicity

will find its way into
the interconnectedness
of all of the Universe
where you already
have so many friends,
and you will find
more who are seeking
you too.
The abundance awaits you.
It's ready to play.
Aphrodite will be
your guide.
She knows what you
are seeking.
She knows why you
are here.
Your willingness
to open to it
will set you free.

FROM: LOVE #19

Wednesday, 17 June 2020

Today I offer you a Rainbow.
You get your Rainbow back.

RED is the color of the rivers of blood swirling
    through your entire body.
        It's the color of the 360° speaker party
        playing high-quality sound.
        It's the red of Lavinia's favorite sweatshirt.
ORANGE is the plump sweetness of
    the ripe mango,
    the melting wax of your homecoming
    candle.
    It's your explosive sumptuousness
    radiating out.
YELLOW is the vibrant fire of enthusiasm.

It's the heat of your life's energy,
the dancing flames of the candles.
GREEN is the luscious leaves of the rain forest,
the hearty grass of the Alpine,
the soft bright moss growing on a
nurse log.
BLUE, it's the cleansing fluidity of winding
water rivulets;
it's the color of the sky after sunset,
when the stars are starting to twinkle;
it's the sound of a single voice
resonating in others' bodies.
Blue is the bowl that holds the food
that has nourished you as you travel.
PURPLE is the lavender oil
dripped into the warm bath water;
it's the lavish new velvety bath towels
to wrap around you;
it's the brilliant light of wisdom
emanating and receiving guidance.
WHITE is the porcelain claw-footed bathtub;
it's the pillar candle, thick and sturdy;
it's the secret passage of the lion.

FROM: LOVE #20

Thursday, 18 June 2020

Welcome to the land
of receptivity
where Love and care
come to you.
Where you don't need
to seek, or work, or ask,
because it's already
yours.
This Love is yours,
and it is with you
every minute of the day,
every second of the night.
You are cherished
You are loved
You are a full rainbow.

Now go rest next
to your pot of gold.

FROM: LOVE #21

viernes, 19 de junio 2020

Querida Chispita,
Hoy te ofrezco
un amor simple
para que descanses
tranquila,
para que sepas
que no tienes que hacer
nada
para ser amada.
te quiero.
te amo.
te adoro.
Así de simple.

FROM: LOVE #21 - Translation

Dear Little Spark,
Today I offer you
a simple love
so you may rest
tranquilly,
so you know
that you don't have to do
anything
to be loved.
I want you.
I love you.
I adore you.
It's that simple.

FROM: LOVE #22

sábado, 20 de junio 2020

Volviendo a la verdad
del amor
pleno y lleno
y floreciendo
dentro de tí,
Hay una energía
fresca, sólida
que refleja
ese crecimiento
de vida pura,
de amor original,
de raíces nuevos.
Ponte a celebrar
este día más largo
como símbolo de

toda la luz que has
dejado entrar en
tu mundo.
Y combínalo con
la fuente infinita
del amor eterno
que tengo para tí.

FROM: LOVE #22 - Translation

Going back to the truth
of love
complete and full
and blooming
inside you,
There is an energy
fresh, solid
that reflects
that growth
of pure life,
of original love,
of new roots.
Celebrate
this longest day

as a symbol of
all the light you have
let enter into
your world.
And combine it with
the infinite source
of eternal love
that I have for you.

FROM: LOVE #23

Sunday, 21 June 2020

Below the star-lit sky
you sit with your feet on
the rocky ground
firmly planted bare
and naked,
fully connected to
who you are.
And I sit with you
full of Love, floaty
and steady, feathery
and straight from
the ashes of the Phoenix,
glowing with the red light,
pulsating as the breeze
blows this fire back

to life.
This will take practice,
this unlearning
of stories,
as you remember
the rainbow of colors
you are made of,
topped
with rose-gold
shimmer

FROM: LOVE #24

Monday, 22 June 2020

Here's to the living question
of Flow...
of how to discern
where the focus needs
to go, to honor
the unfolding dreams
and those who are
connected to them.
Bubble Rainbow Magic
and conversations
in the grass,
Amazon salutes
from Harlem,
winding green pathways
of discovery

and purple hearts
that float to the
Pacific Ocean
while laughter from there
circles down under
to warm the
start of winter
with a cup of hot tea.
A day of weaving
Love, a day
of loving flow.
You know where
the focus needs
to go....

FROM: LOVE #25

Tuesday, 23 June 2020

I love your dark blue nails
and the fact that
your underwear matches
your olive-green shirt
that incorporates
highlights of burnt orange
and a complementary blue
to the fingernails
and the shorts of a lighter shade.
I love the flow of color,
the texture of pattern.
I love your attention to detail,
inside and out,
just for fun,
not for show,

but for the pure joy in
visual stimulation
and playful design.

FROM: LOVE #26

Mercredi, 24 Juin 2020

Je t'offre une main
pour tenir dans
la tienne,
toujours là
disponible
pour toi à travers
quoi que ce soit.
Je peux même changer
de forme pour que
tu en aïs une de chaque
côté, quand tu en as
besoin.
Je sais que tu es
forte, courageuse, maligne,
et capable.

Mais je veux aussi que tu sache
que tu n'es jamais seule,
et je te connais assez bien
pour savoir
que tu es très drôle
quand tu te sens bien.
Alors, on pleur ?
ou on rigole ?
De toute façon
Je suis là.

FROM: LOVE #26 - Translation

I offer you a hand
to hold in
yours,
always there
available
for you through
anything.
I can even change
form so that
you have one on each
side, whenever you may

need it.
I know you are
strong, courageous, clever,
and capable.
But I also want you to know
that you are never alone,
and I know you well enough
to know
how funny you are
when you feel good.
So, are we crying?
or are we laughing?
Either way
I'm here.

FROM: LOVE #27

Thursday, 25 June 2020

There is nothing
in this world
that matters more
than the love
I have for you.
I know you're exhausted
and you're raging
and you can't
transform fast enough,
and there are so many
urgent issues that
need tending to.
But this love I need
to get to you?
It's urgent too.

Today.
Right now.
This is no longer
optional.
It's part of what
keeps you whole and
full.
This Love is the
essence of who
you are,
in flow,
in pause,
in breath.
Relax – it's ok
to open
your heart
and feel the
purity, the fire,
the depth
of what calls you.

FROM: LOVE #28

Friday, 26 June 2020

The connection held
throughout the
time you were traveling
to distant lands
and maintained
a fluidity
of wisdom and care
highlighted
your capacity
to learn
to evolve
to grow,
or rather
to return
to ground

and align
with who you were
and are again –
a source of Love.
Welcome Home.

FROM: LOVE #29

Saturday, 27 June 2020

There is a brightness
emerging
with the fresh color
that is coming
back to life
from within.
I'm writing this
poem to
water your secret garden
with Love
and ensure that
it does not go
thirsty.
Your inner
blooming inspires

more creativity
in how to nourish the soil
how to grow the roots
stimulate the senses
stoke the fire
talk to the plants
sing with the birds
listen to the Angels
go with the flow,
and offer this Love
that only you can feel
in your own way.
It's available
for you all day
today.
Tomorrow's new Love
will find you
in a different
form.

FROM: LOVE #30

Sunday, 28 June 2020

Regardless of what transpired today
I'm still inclined to want to say
with my whole heart, "I love you, Lei!"

There's not a piece that's missing here.
Your wholeness speaks above the fear
and momentum's mounting, that is clear.

This Love is growing with your practice
and each time you listen, the bare fact is
LOVE seeks all it can to back this

beautiful voyage to make it known
that you've a curiosity for Love full blown.
The doors are opening, the birds have flown

to warn the Angels up above
and the Cupid and the dove
that Lei is out to discover Love!

We join forces now for you
to get an extra dose or two
of this juicy Love so true

Delivered to your bedroom door
Never done like this before
To ensure your faith's restored.

With this then, we can end winning
Though it was a rough beginning
Love's now getting thick, not thinning.

Rest, my precious, in your knowing
that I love you; you are glowing.
There, that's better, back to flowing.

FROM: LOVE #31

Monday, 29 June 2020

From a day full of delight
to being here with you tonight,
it has been such a great pleasure
swinging on the porch in leisure,

after working with such care
clearing out the space and air
with white sage and Palo Santo
and the rhythms of the cantos

from Brasil to Harpers Ferry
eating mangos and dark cherries.
Now you really have moved in,
setting yourself up to win.

I am feeling so inspired
even if you're really tired.
I know that my Love is true,
an' I can give it all to you.

There is plenty to go 'round,
but what a special heart I found.
Let this Love grow with the moon.
I will catch you if you swoon.

FROM: LOVE #32

Tuesday, 30 June 2020

What if I loved you for real?
I mean, not just sayin',
but it's really how I feel.
What if I were playin',
and playin' *was* the even keel?

What if it all weren't so serious?
and we could laugh a lot,
enjoying the mysterious
while developing the plot.

What if we could do this on the ocean
or in pilgrimage along the coast,
getting movement into motion
"I'll take coffee with my toast."

Right? There's a gypsy in your heart.
She's dynamic and ever-flowing.
I love the way she's living art, and
love that she is always growing.

How about we keep on dreaming,
open to the quantum field
where all the highest comes in streaming,
and true love and goodness yield.

FROM: LOVE #33

Wednesday, 1 July 2020

I pace myself to your heartbeat --
listening to when it shifts,
sensing its acceleration,
noticing when it might need holding,
and relishing times it calmly sings.
Tonight, there is a depth of joy
emerging from the wells of Love
you kept hidden inside
that gurgled quietly
along their underground path,
until they came to an
opening in the rock,
where they trickled through
as steady as the source they came from.
Your heart aligns with ease,

because it knows these waters.
It knows they come with the full energy
of a spring,
with swirls that move through rocks,
and with the spontaneity that adapts
to what they meet.
Your heart also knows that,
just like these waters will transform
into sea and clouds and rain,
it too will transform in
mysterious ways to its own
magical shapes of Love.

FROM: LOVE #34

Thursday, 2 July 2020

I am here to join the
warmth of summer
and sunshine on your
turquoise-tipped bare feet,
to let you know you can
let your guard down here.
So maybe you're mad, Chispita,
or even exasperated.
That's ok too.
I'm not giving up on you.
Maybe today the story
brings you fury, frustration,
stuckness.
These will not last.
My love, though, that

is here now,
and it will be here
after they are gone.
This love will go
on and on and on...

FROM: LOVE #35

Friday, 3 July 2020

The wine berries
you picked today
were red, in the
classic color of Love,
but I will tell you
that my love for you
is a lot more fun
than just one color.

The love I feel for you
is of adventure
and exploration,
of rainbows after storms,
of unknown rivers,
and weather systems,

of gold and glitter,
unexpected laughter,
and creative solutions
that give you pause
to the brilliance behind
the uncanny outcomes.

I am of the mystery
that will carry you
to those magical places
that leave you breathless,
only because you are
inspired at the deepest
level of your being
to let go and enjoy
the fullness of
this moment.

In this moment, I love you.
And this will lead to the
next moment, in which
I love you,
and the next...
We will discover where this
Love leads us...

Wherever you go,
I will be there with you,
Loving you
wholly, fully,
as seen by the tattoo
on my left shoulder.

FROM: LOVE #36

Samedi, 4 Juillet 2020

Viens t'asseoir
pour colorier.
Laisse les autres,
et viens t'asseoir
avec moi.

Ici tu es à l'abri.
Nous générons la gentillesse aimante
et on veut la bonté
pour tous
même ceux qu'on
ne comprend pas.

Ici tu as et tu auras toujours
ta place à la table,

et accès à toutes les couleurs
de l'arc en ciel.
Ici tu as la bienveillance, c'est sûr.

FROM: LOVE #36 - Translation

Come and sit down
to color.
Leave the others
and come sit down
with me.

Here you are safe.
We generate loving kindness
and we want goodness
for everyone
even those we
do not understand.

Here you have and you will always have
your place at the table,
and access to all colors
of the rainbow.
Here you have benevolence, for sure.

FROM: LOVE #37

Sunday, 5 July 2020

I see the work you put into
your "path"
that is really this non-linear
experience of
quantum leaps
across multiple dimensions
of time.
The core of it though
is the discovery
of LOVE,
in all its essence,
it's full expression,
it's magnificent potential.
You know this is
why you are here.

You know the difference
between inclusion and
discernment.
You were July-born in
the summer of LOVE,
and this July we are
back in conversation.
You know I speak
through you, Aphrodite.
Welcome, my dear beauty.
There is much to talk about.
There is much Love to share.
Today I celebrate
your return with the full moon
to your full self.
It's ok to go Big.
I will be Big with you.
We will be together,
In LOVE.

FROM: LOVE #38

Monday, 6 July 2020

YES! Yeah!
You got it!
LOVE is in the air
LOVE is in the closet!
LOVE is everywhere
LOVE is in the pause, it
is in the foundation
and is the most essential.
You're recognizing LOVE
as key to your potential.
I saw you cross a threshold
today in all your beauty.
Your fullness is now tenfold
no longer starved by duty.
I'm here to stay the course with you

though others may resist.
And since we both know what is true
your worries can desist.
The world around you needs this LOVE
that you are generating.
The Earth below and Sky above
have no more use for hating.
It harms the heart and eats the Soul
and undermines our pureness
when what we need is to be whole.
Of that there's only sureness.
So welcome to your new horizon.
You have earned your keep.
We get to celebrate with eyes on
Oneness as we sleep.

FROM: LOVE #39

Tuesday, 7 July 2020

I am here for your protection
and to offer you direction.
After many magic places,
new terrain with unknown faces,
all for service to community
and your wish for feeling unity,
I'm appreciating your capacity,
bravery, courage, and tenacity.
These as well will serve you now.
Your biggest question here is, "How?"
With your heart I know you'll listen
I can see you start to glisten
with the sweat from your hard work.
See, with Love there is a perk!
You are backed by a deep wisdom

and the colors from the prism.
Though there's more you cannot see,
more to learn and more to be,
I am proud of where you are.
You have really come so far.
Grateful you are on our team,
Happy that you get to dream,
for it's cuz you have crossed over
that you're sitting now in clover.
Rest assured it's a good move.
Hallelujah! Now let's groove.

FROM: LOVE #40

Wednesday, 8 July 2020

In full song,
you step up the
invisible stairs
that lead to a
new plateau
where fresh views
of the theater
give insights
to the goings on
back stage.
You sit down
and chew on the
food for thought
with the new tooth
you just got today.

You have found
nourishment
in unexpected places
from unexpected people
and with surprising results –
You are not crazy,
not tarnished.
You are just getting started,
so loveable,
so sane.

FROM: LOVE #41

Jeudi, 9 Juillet 2020

Bravo, ma chérie!
Tu es libre.
Tu as traversé la frontière,
et tu as tes pieds firmes
de l'autre côté.
Depuis le terrain vidé
à Hiroshima, jusqu'à
ton jardin secret, tu as
mis en place les plantes,
soigné la terre,
arrosé, et complété
les grands nettoyages
finaux, et maintenant
tu peux commencer
à construire.

Ta fondation est saine.
Tes racines prennent.
Et tout ce que tu veux
observer – dans le panier !
Tu es brave, honnête, et la
pureté te donne la clarté.
Et pour ça, tu as des amis
qui t'aiment.
Petit à petit, tu grandis.
Tu te renforces,
tu te reconstruis,
et je suis avec toi.

FROM: LOVE #41 - Translation

Bravo my dear!
You are free.
You crossed the border,
and you have your feet firm
on the other side.
From the emptied ground
in Hiroshima, to
your secret garden, you have
set up the plants,

cared for the earth,
watered, and completed
the big final
cleanings, and now
you can begin
to build.
Your foundation is healthy.
Your roots are taking.
And whatever you want
observe - in the basket!
You are brave, honest, and the
purity gives you clarity.
And for that, you have friends
who love you.
Little by little, you grow.
You strengthen yourself,
you rebuild yourself,
and I am with you.

FROM: LOVE #42

Friday, 10 July 2020

My Love 4U is eternal.
It shines with authenticity,
is grounded in integrity,
and rooted with wisdom.
I flow in and out of clock time
on my own rhythm,
interconnected with yours,
as you continue to seek clarity.
Your unstoppability
prevails through the confusion
the fear, the aloneness, the
grief of times past,
and through the guidance,
the openings, the support
and release of times present.

Your night time wanderings
land you on the warm
wet rock slab
after the second wave
of rain showers
as you come out from
under the tree
and make your way
home
to me.

FROM: LOVE #43

Samedi, 11 Juillet 2020

L'amour d'aujourd'hui
vient du centre de la planète,
nourri par le soleil même,
et éblouissant dans
sa brillance.
Il monte à travers
tes racines pour te
nourrir directement,
pour que tu puisses te
sentir pleine, inspirée
aimée, valorisée,
appréciée, soignée,
et remplie de bonté.
Il monte aussi à travers
les rochers et se

trouve dans tous les petits
baies de vin rouge
que tu as cueilli
et que tu mangeras demain matin
pour le petit déjeuner.

FROM: LOVE #43 - Translation

Today's Love
comes from the center of the planet,
nourished by the very sun,
and dazzling in
its brilliance.
She rises through
your roots to
feed you directly,
so that you can
feel full, inspired
loved, valued,
appreciated, cared for,
and filled with goodness.
She also rises through
the rocks and is
found in all the little

red wine berries
that you picked
and that you will eat tomorrow morning
for breakfast.

FROM: LOVE #44

Sunday, 12 July 2020

You say you're surprised
I'm still here, writing you.
Well, this Love has surmised
that the fear is all through.

Not the kind that keeps you well protected
but the stuff that leaves you disconnected
It's important to notice the difference.
The former will offer deliverance.

The latter is but an illusion
that'll lead you to faulty conclusions.
When fear works with Love as a guardian divine
to open awareness and give you a sign

You'll know you're aligned with the highest.
Collaboration is always the flyest.
It brings out the best, and highlights connection
that ultimately now is the human direction.

So yes, my Dear Lei, I am here
Celebrating your new version of fear.
And all that aside, what I'm learning
Is I write you to fill a deep yearning.

It's got nothing to do with achievement
and rather, enjoys the appeasement.
Your presence allows my expression
of a Love fresh and pure without question.

FROM: LOVE #45

Monday, 13 July 2020

I'm leaning now towards a kick in the pants
with the loving idea of giving a chance
to your most brilliant self to fly and to flourish
while relating to others who are happy
> to nourish
your dreams, your truths, your badass approach,
your ability to become the transformational
> coach
who inspires and guides and creates the
> container.
It's all for the best, really, it's a no-brainer!
I know you are worried to live in duality,
but you get to decide on your own damn reality.
The option is there if you choose to explore it.
You might even find that you will adore it.

It's time for releasing the mess of the past,
sending full loving kindness and blessings to last
the rest of your days and others' as well.
You'll see the results – you never can tell.
What I know is I love you and know you
    are able
to earn the respect for a space at the table.
There's a brilliance inside you that needs
    to come out.
I will say it again; one day I may shout,
but for now I'll be gentle since it's the
    first time,
that I urge you to action in this little rhyme.

FROM: LOVE #46

Tuesday, 14 July 2020

The stars in the sky above
shine down on your lighted path.
The glitter in the pavement
shines upward in celebration.
You can take off your protective jacket
because your discernment is powerful enough
that you know what you need
and what you do not.
The cosmos is with you.
The fireflies echo their enthusiasm.
I am thrilled at the prospect
that you are even more whole
today than yesterday;
that your pureness fills you,
that the house-cleaning is

shifting your very being.
With every day you practice,
your brilliance brightens,
your balance steadies,
your wisdom deepens,
your depth widens,
and my love for you
expands
into the infinite.

FROM: LOVE #47

Wednesday, 15 July 2020

If you could see me,
you would see my broad smile,
the twinkle in my eyes,
the raised eyebrows,
and the perked cheekbones.
You would see me leaning
back in my chair,
cocking my head sideways
so I can get a better look
at you
as I soak in your creativity.
There's something opening up
that I haven't seen before –
a "you"- ness that
is showing herself

and coming out to play.
And what I find most
delightful is your
surprise when you
discover that others
might want to play
with you too –
just like me,
I come back to play
every day
because I love the
newness I encounter
every time I find you.

FROM: LOVE #48

Thursday 16 July 2020

There is a freshness
in your step this morning
infused by the summer breeze
of the night
flowing gently through spaces
and finding new pockets
of energy
that bounce with you
as you awaken.
I'm here to greet you
this morning
to wish you a beautiful day
of preparations
for your journey
with your Mum.

Only you will know
that I am with you
unless others notice the glow
that comes from the
rose-gold shimmer
we are nourishing
inside you.
But all I care is that
you know.
You know I'm with you
through every present moment,
Ready to flow
in any direction
we are called to.

FROM: LOVE #49

Friday, 17 July 2020

Wherever you are,
Whatever you're feeling
is okay.
You have done enough today.
Rest in the Love
I am wrapping around you.
Rest in the knowing
you are in good company.
Rest with the clarity
of the field
even as the voices
around the woods
continue with their banter.
You can let go
and relax into the night sky

with the fireflies.
Let the annihilation, the rage,
the grief, the disrespect
of the morning
float away into the trees
letting the world transform
the energy into
potential.
Even if you are discouraged,
you gave with your full heart,
and I will refill it
with goodness as you sleep.

FROM: LOVE #50

Saturday, 18 July 2020

The calm confidence of flow
suits you well.
When you settle in what you know,
I can tell
you are expanding your awareness.
Every moment
you are present,
the magic
unfolds in response.
Today it delivers you
up to the comet
at Spruce Knob.
Others too are looking for
the cosmic sight
across the celestial

Heavens.
What a delightful
thrill it is with your Mum!
Today's been full –
the lake, the blueberries
the campsite, the comet.
The food has been
stupendous.
Keep letting go,
it's precious.

FROM: LOVE #51

Sunday, 19 July 2020

As we sit in pink chairs
by the lake,
next to your Mum,
the darkened night sky stretches
over the daisies and the milkweed.
While anticipating the celestial resplendence,
I am celebrating the day
you just lived
with ease and relaxation...
In the morning, waking peacefully to the light rain
and dozing back to dreamy sleep,
then re-awakening as the dancing clouds
moved through to other places.
In the afternoon, finding ways to figure out

a place to walk,
and landing the welcoming magical
Eliza Trail.
It led you to moseying up the fern-lined creek,
picnic-pausing in the grassy meadow,
and meandering along the luscious green ridge
down to the trickling creek
you both lay beside,
face-up to the light green
susurrating canopy.
"They have a lot to talk about!"
she chortled.
You walked
through the forest
squishing the mud through your toes,
leading to the casual denouement
along the dirt road
with Gandy Creek-cleansed feet.
All in stride.
What a day of summer scents
Summer breeze
Summer ease
Gentle pace.
There was love in every moment -
Relaxed, breezy

Pleasant, easy
Leisurely, majestic
Fun, magical
and the smells, the summer smells
of spruce, plants, fresh air...
Bringing us back to now, sitting in
the pink chairs
on the West end of Spruce Knob Lake.
The night's arrival is bringing its own magic,
the darkness its own peace,
the sky its own dazzling show.
You can rest and enjoy
the unguarded beauty,
elegant fullness,
graceful motion,
and heavenly blessing
of the wholeness
of this moment
together.

FROM: LOVE #52

Monday, 20 July 2020

Dearest Lavinia
Yes! Yes!
Get up ! Get out !
Pull up ! Pull out !
I see the wisdom
in your urgent call
to get out of the hell
they bring to you,
in your own dwelling,
where, though they are visitors,
they speak *for* you
in front of you, as if you
aren't there,
Where they talk about you
as if you

were a child,
as if they
knew better than you
what you need.
Where they put you on display
to be judged
like an animal in a zoo,
pretending all the while
that they are bathing you
with praise.
The rage that comes
with the cumulative
annihilation consumes your heart,
your insides,
your very being.
The amount of energy it requires
to be seen, heard, acknowledged
is inordinate.
And so I see why
sometimes it's best
to let it all go.
Let yourself go. Let the story go.
Let them all go.
And sink instead
into the wisdom that

is unaffected by any of it
No need for reflection.
No need for meaning.
No need for struggle.
Only a deep connection
to all that is.
And in that place
So deep, so pure,
I am holding a space for you
of Love
of Reverence
of Deliverance.

FROM: LOVE #53

Tuesday, 21 July 2020

Let yourself melt into
the softness
of the velvet clouds
ready to take you
across the new sky
you have reached
through pure determination,
supported by loving hands
and open hearts.
Close your eyes
and enter the
Secret Garden of Love
I have been tending
to receive you,
and feel the gentle care

I offer to soothe
your liberated spaces
as Love replaces the pain
that once resided there

FROM: LOVE #54

Wednesday, 22 July 2020

Oooh how the Universe like to play !
And you are learning to find your way !
Today's events are really bold
The way the parallels unfold
through connections far and wide
so many subtleties could hide,
but speaking of them brings them out
and celebrations are about
the ways that synthesis has found
the best idea for sovereign's sound

through the engine of a Beetle
with the precision of a needle!
Saban, he is a Diplomat,
plus he's from the Navy, that

brings two details of yours
into these uncanny shores
And just like the Poster Rey,
He's from Turkey, "Wow! No way!"
And the numbers added up
Speak of Freedom. Let's stand up!

Driving home the crescent moon
Beckoned songs of a new tune.
These are times of new dimension
Set in motion by intention
I'm am loving that you listened
To your instinct unconditioned
in its purity divine
fully focused to align
with the means to give support
to success in Love's report.

Nicely done within a day
That you shifted in display
Your new story into now
I'm amazed at the Big How !

FROM: LOVE #55

Thursday, 23 July 2020

When your heart opens unexpectedly
and you can't hold back the excitement,

when you have the sense that "yes"
is all you could answer
and everything falls away,

when you find connection
through synchronicity
and the flow feels joyful and effortless,

when you can feel that with this step
something magical is happening
and you have no idea
where it will lead you,

when you feel a sense of belonging
and that there is still hope,

when you find yourself asking,
"Wow, could this really be?"
and the more you open to it,
the more alive you feel,

when you are deeply satisfied
by this new step because it fills
your whole being,
and you know somehow
you are on track...

This is the time of new beginnings
and the kind of leap that shifts
your whole life
and brings you home
to yourself.

FROM: LOVE #56

Friday, 24 July 2020

On this double-rainbow
Love-filled day
I celebrate your coming out
to sail by Love Point and
meet life
in all its abundance,
so that you can participate
as the salty sailor
of your treasure-hunting
dreams.
Having weathered
some dark n stormies
that honed your nav skills,
you can open your imagination
to possibility, to choice,

to freedom.
Blessed be your connection
to all that is,
and all that you discover
with great aplomb
on our quest for
generating conditions for you
to thrive.
Like walking a labyrinth
it will bring you back
to center,
back to wandering,
back to Love,
and on to more exploration !
Happy Birthday
I love you
Dear Chispita Chérie

FROM: LOVE #57

Samedi, 25 Juillet 2020

Avant que tu dormes
au clair de la lune
et que les étoiles
te chantent ses berceuses,
j'ajoute un petit mot d'amour
pour que tu saches que
je suis fière de toi.
Les résultats parlent
pour eux mêmes,
les rêves aussi.
Je te souhaite tout le courage
pour que tu puisse rester
connecté au pourquoi –
du grand système d'amour
dans lequel tu as une capacité

et tu es douée.
Rêve librement.
Maintenant tu peux lâcher,
et en lâchant, tout
tombera
en place
pour toi.

FROM: LOVE #57 - Translation

Before you sleep
in the moonlight
and that the stars
sing their lullabies to you,
I add a little love note
so that you know that
I am proud of you.
The results speak
for themselves,
the dreams do too.
I wish you all the courage
so that you can stay
connected to the why -
of the great love system

in which you have an ability
and you are skilled.
Dream freely.
Now you can let go
and by letting go, everything
will fall
in place
for you.

FROM: LOVE #58

Sunday, 26 July 2020

I am here to remind you tonight
That you are worthy of love alright.
Worthy of the knowledge you have sown,
Worthy of the skills you have honed,
Worthy of sailing the salty seas,
Worthy of breathing the ocean breeze.

You may struggle with this knowing.
It's ok, I'll still be showing
How much Love I have for you.
It's abundant, and it's true,
Wrap you in it so you feel
That this Love is fully real.

Grounding now, it's time to rest
with the anchor that holds best
In the core that you have found
With the many friends around.
Let us settle into sleep, with
Restful breaths and Love so deep.

FROM: LOVE #59

Monday, 27 July 2020

Even if you don't believe yet
You meet me every day
and bring your pure intention
of discovery to the conversation.
You listen with innocence
for what you long to hear
from me,
and I meet you here too,
tuning in to your heart
to sense how the day's
present message may emerge.
Today you took a step
aligned with your sovereignty –
of a sporty, fun, stylie, elegant
classy and gorgeous life

energy that is also
practical, grounded and
strong.
The connections you are
building with others now, from
your core of Love to theirs
matches the alignment
of the bigger picture
and opens a collaboration
you hadn't imagined
was possible.
I'm here to confirm
these connections are real.
Your feelings are too.
You are emerging
in your own flavor
your own sound
your own taste
as an original
source of
LOVE.

FROM: LOVE #60

Tuesday, 28 July 2020

I am here.
Always here.
Here with you.
Here in the flow.
Beauty is here,
so is connection,
and safety too.
They follow my guidance.
They bloom with the buds.
And you, as the bee,
You build bridges
between entities
otherwise disconnected.
As the flower, you receive
replenishment and

satisfaction that you
are part of a bigger whole.
A bigger life.
And as the nectar,
you're the liquid love
that can transform
in endless ways.
The water waves,
The Earth grounds,
the soft breeze blows,
and you relax,
wrapped in this
blanket of love,
into the eternal energy
renewing with
every moment.

FROM: LOVE #61

Wednesday, 29 July 2020

Singing, you find the sound
that brings dance to motion.
Dancing, you play with the
rhythm that shimmers through
your graceful arms.
Looking, you discover the edges
of where your world can expand
beyond its current
images, into the invisible
mystery that holds
the magic you can only
sense into, but you know is reliable
in its loyalty and creativity.
Together there is connection
to the shared vision

of explorative expression,
and an interpretation
that honors each
unique combination of
horizons.
In this depth, I (Love)
wind my way joyfully
through the metaphors
to discover all the
different ways
I can play with you.

FROM: LOVE #62

Thursday, 30 July 2020

I love you from above;
I love you from below;
I stretch with your Desire
As far as it will go.

These days there's so much clearing;
I'm filling it with Love.
I wonder if you've gotten
the message from the dove?

The peace she brings is gentle.
It's soothing and sincere.
With Love from different angles,
the energy is clear.

You're blessed with many allies.
They love you just like me.
As you begin to open,
You'll realize what CAN BE.

FROM: LOVE #63

Friday, 31 July 2020

I've seen the rage
that engulfs you
in the repetition
of invisible patterns
that have crept inside
your mind and body,
the poison oozing
through your breath
and closing your throat.
But I sense an opening lightness
in the way you're moving now,
your freshly-shaven silky legs
with their new desire to
run again.
I know I'm not

the only one
who loves you.
And maybe this shift
can offer momentum
to build your
world of Love,
expanding with you
and your free agents,
just like the ones
you met with
today.

FROM: LOVE #64

Saturday, 1 August 2020

The beauty of your Pirate Love
is immaculate.
It's born in the wildness
of the ocean,
the steadiness of the waves,
and the bling of the treasures
you can find along
the way of your
expedition of discovery.
Purple, gold, sparkly.
They are all part of the
party of life
that invites you
into brilliance,
expansion and

humble extravagance,
as you deepen
the wisdom that
will hold it all
into perspective.
Blessings be to the
Love I feel for you
in connection to
all of this.

FROM: LOVE #65

Sunday, 2 August 2020

Please don't give up
Love's filling your cup
I am your witness
There is a richness
You are tapping into
an' I know you'll get through
to the next level
No need to settle.
The winds are a'changing
The luck's rearranging.
It's all in your favor
You may choose the flavor
Stay open to the mystery
Regardless of history
The quantum is here

Let Magic appear
or show you a sign
on how to align
with this Love so hearty
I'll throw you a party
with the moon in the sky
and the oreo pie
the sailboat be bringing
the music & singing
the joy and the laughter
the drying off after
the dive in the water
and cooling the hotter
left from the day's sun
The night has begun
The darkness and pleasure
The chest full of treasure
It showed you the heart
That glowed from the start
And it will continue
to grow Love within you
With boldness and fun,
I love you a ton.

FROM: LOVE #66

Monday, 3 August 2020

Here we are in a transition,
Partly from what u been wishin',
Present to a new existence,
Opening to Love's assistance,
Helping with how to discern
What's essential to be learned.
You are both a part of nature,
and apart, a single creature...
How interconnection binds you
While inner connection finds you.
Power's in this paradox,
Opening the 3D box,
Two sides of a flying coin,
Parallel realities join.
It's the "both," "yes," "and" of ALL,

In the space parts float and fall.
Flow dynamics, always moving,
Growing, changing, sometimes blooming.
Beauty in connected whole -
Wholeness in the separate beauty -
Both are true, and let your soul
Find its place and shake some booty.

FROM: LOVE #67

Tuesday, 4 August 2020

I too sometimes have quiet times
when silence in its wisdom chimes.

Instead of words to speak of Love,
just being with you I think of

your vibrant essence shining out.
It says so much, no need to shout.

I love to be right by your side
and sense into the deep and wide.

Together there's a combination
unique to you for the duration

of this precious life you're living,
full of Love, which I'll keep giving.

Either way, I love your presence.
It brings delight and gentle pleasance.

It's enough for me today
to simply BE with my dear Lei.

FROM: LOVE #68

Wednesday, 5 August 2020

The swirl of turmoil that
is the clearing flow
of energy past
blows open the space
for the sea to rise into.
And as this full-moon tide
of clean Love fills
the empty pockets
that once held stories
stuck in their old pain,
it releases them into the
whirling waters that
will feed other
creatures and revive
in new forms of life.

The rainbow of love
shines colorful light
through the moving
turquoise currents,
creating a festive result
of new patterns,
new designs,
original shapes & shades,
and a plethora
of giddy joy,
because you know
we did this together,
in love,
with love,
as love.

FROM: LOVE #69

Thursday, 6 August 2020

I love your little red dress.
Its suits the curve of your smile
and highlights your painted red nails.

I love its classic finesse;
It flairs with a fabulous style,
and sports the most wondrous details.

It's festive and charming and bold,
could go to a party of fair.
A parade would also behold
its magical breath of fresh air.

Today I love it on *you!*
There's something about how you've changed -

Another portal gone through,
and stories are all rearranged.

The joy, love, and peace from inside
are matching the dress's complexion.
Your presence can no longer hide.
You're off in a whole new direction.

I'm happy to celebrate seeing
the effort you've given commitment,
to opening new ways of being
that offer you living fulfillment.

So, dance in your dress and rejoice;
The party is just getting started.
The welcoming freedom and choice
for true love and goodness whole-hearted.

FROM: LOVE #70

Friday, 7 August 2020

When it comes to having a natural 6th sense,
the capacity you have is truly immense,
Over and over, you've seen it play out,
doesn't matter the cause or what it's about.
The mystery's there & you'll never know how
you know what to do, and when is the "now."

With Jenny & Bill today as examples,
it's important to see their value as samples.
The service and care that you can provide
has power and wonder that can't be denied.
So why are you stalling to write to the women
when LOVE is awaiting your gift to be given?

I'm writing to urge you to act by tomorrow.
An' if you're still blocked, you're welcome to borrow
some power from me, to support your succeeding
in writing the invite and start with proceeding
to build up the love boat and find the free agents
who'll enter the magic with splendor & patience.

You'll have so much fun in joining together.
Your boat will sail well, no matter the weather.
I'm here with you now to assure and encourage,
for it's the next step to
FOLLOW YOUR MISSION!

FROM: LOVE #71

Saturday, 8 August 2020

The hug I'm sending to you now
is the kind that
warms your heart
settles the nerves
softens the breathing
soothes the worry
comforts the doubt
obliterates judgment
acknowledges anxiety
recognizes your courage
celebrates your risk-taking
knows how hard you've worked
understands your mission
adores your presence
Holds you in

full
deep
pure
LOVE
and all you gotta do
is open to receive

FROM: LOVE #72

Sunday, 9 August 2020

Whether the words come out or not,
I love you just the same.
Whether your tears flow cold or hot,
I'm really glad you came
to sit with me again tonight;
I miss you when you're gone.
I really want to make it right
and fix it before dawn.
The blues you've had throughout the day
have left you without words,
But all my Love is here to stay;
I'll sing it with the birds.
Go quiet if you so desire;
I know your fire inside.
The crickets join us in the choir

We'll keep a steady stride.
So don't you worry 'bout this poem,
for it will write itself.
Just stick with us, and we will show'em
You're not meant for the shelf.
You can step out from your hiding;
I will hold your hand.
With my Love I'll be abiding
by your bold new stand.

FROM: LOVE #73

Monday, 10 August 2020

What if we could start the day
with celebrating Love for Lei?

What if we could set the tone,
assuring that you're not alone?

What if you could change beliefs
to those that give you most relief,
and settle into LOVE as given
every day to keep you driven?

Moving now with Love through time,
you're getting strong with each day's climb.
Bouncing forward like a kanga
Superpowers of a manga

Let's keep going day by day,
Making sure there's time to play.
Just as long as LOVE's a part,
I'll share with you my generous heart.

FROM: LOVE #74

Tuesday, 11 August 2020

You get to need
    Whatever you need.
No call to justify
No judge to question why
Balance in the picture bigger
than the story's trigger.
No one needs to understand
What is under every strand, or
what's the link between each doubt.
We just need to get them out,
Blast'em with a dose of Love
or Raspberry Chocolove.
Something that will help you dance
Shake into that second chance
Keep on going towards the magic

Mystery that's bright, not tragic
That's where all your friends reside;
That's how we electric slide
into unknown territories
styling graceful categories.
Yes, we got this, we are one,
All the allies here for fun.
Evolution, that's our mission.
Love plus Love, that's our addition.
Call it good, cuz it's for real,
Love is with you, that's the deal.

FROM: LOVE #75

Wednesday, 12 August 2020

As the water, you move with the wind,
your flow adapting to the coasts
you encounter, your rise and fall
synchronizing with the moon.

As the coast you weave in and out
of waterlines, rising high to meet
the ever-changing sky,
reaching deep into the Earth.

As the bridge between worlds
you hold the balance
moving with ease along the edges
offering an alternative way to cross.

As Love you expand potential
Fearless in your stance
Tenacious in your tenderness
Opening to higher ways of being.

FROM: LOVE #76

Thursday, 13 August 2020

I am with you in the stubborn ruts of doubt
The grooves that keep you rigid
Those self-defying boxes that stack
to form walls you can't see over.
I see your mind in the pacing
it takes on, like an animal held captive.
Call it patterns, call it past.
The rage seethes out in the form of resentment,
then turns inward in self pity,
because it can't find a clear way out.
Feeling as though in the cumulative effects
you will either implode, or explode,
or both.
This too is part of your journey.
This too will liberate you, even in its

illusion of stuckness.
There is momentum still, slow and hot, like
a lava sea underneath the Earth's crust.
The rage is not you, however.
It is an energy without words
that carries tremendous power,
and that you are deeply attuned to.
It was your home for so long.
The familiarity deceives you in its
false comfort combined with the cheerful
"making the best of a situation."
I am with you there,
but it is not where you belong.
I am with you there,
because otherwise you might believe
it's all true.
I am with you there,
so you can see the contrast,
and so I can remind you
what resonance feels like -
Deep down in your core,
so you can come back home,
to Love.

FROM: LOVE #77

Friday, 14 August 2020

Coconut caramel salted crunch
My love today for you, is like a fruit punch.
It's colorful and fresh, and full of bubbles too.
It's made for you to share, and also just for you.
A party in a bowl to celebrate now,
the poetry of Love, explored with "She Pow"!
The ladies all came through with caring
    whole-hearted;
I loved the conversation, we finally got it
    started!
Hooray for this beginning, it opens up a door.
We'll find some other ways to do it plenty more.
The key is in connection, Love moves a
    different way
to generate community and open space to play.

With beaming satisfaction, I sense a new potential
This topic of true Love for you is most essential.

FROM: LOVE #78

Saturday, 15 August 2020

I offer all my tenderness
to hug your whole self
so that even the pieces
we still need to recover
know they are not abandoned,
know they are loved,
and know that in the
secret garden home of
coastal sailing, fire spinning
delicious foods and flowers,
music, laughter, art
colorful funny friends
and relaxing excellence,
they have a place
that they belong,

and they will always be welcome.
All of you belongs
in this LOVE HUG
of liberation and wholeness.

FROM: LOVE #79

Sunday, 16 August 2020

As the accordion of time
expands and contracts
with the melody of
unfolding songs telling
stories of triumphs and
tribulations,
your baby steps fall
into their own rhythm,
yet still aware of how
they are moving with the chorus.
There is a delicate
balance you are exploring –
between depth and integration,
between width and specifics,
discovering all the while

the ever-presence of stillness,
the reliability of LOVE,
and the power of alignment.
There is chaos in the mix,
but we are going steady,
strengthening with practice,
lightening with release,
and softening with forgiveness.
It's time to land,
and I am landing with you.
All about that base,
that Love.
No trouble.*

*by surprise, I landed on a reference to Meghan Trainor's song, "All About That Bass." Kevin Kadish: Epic Records, 2014. Single.

FROM: LOVE #80

Monday, 17 August 2020

Today's Love is soft
like the white blanket
that brings you warmth
whether crumpled or wrapped;
like the feathery clouds
that greeted you this morning
across a delicate blue sky.
Soft like the melting nectarine
in your mouth topping the
chia porridge of the early morn.
Soft like the gentle pressure
of my hand, full of compassion,
on your sore lower back.
Today is soft because
we're wrapping up the lunar month –

a month of diving and clearing
A month of releasing and grieving;
wrapping up to start afresh
tomorrow
with the new moon
Bringing with us the new beginnings
we have also gleaned
of birthdays and bareboat nations
of VB8 and integrations.
Jalan, Jalan we walk along,
Soro, Soro our steady song.

FROM: LOVE #81

Tuesday, 18 August 2020

Though you may not feel it,
I know you're still in there.
You are still bigger than
any pain you will find inside.
Your natural state is that
which holds it all,
that which holds perspective,
that which knows, like me,
that you will endure.
It is that which honors the
deepest level of your being.
It's the fierce and steady force
that is connected to the whole.
Breathe freely, knowing
that I see you,

even when you can't see
yourself.

FROM: LOVE #82

Wednesday, 19 August 2020

The pitter patter of the gentle
early rain is to bring
peace to your soft morning
to start the day with a
slow graceful opening,
not too bright, not too stormy,
just an easeful introduction
to your day
so that you may find
serenity, calm, and balance
at your own pace.

FROM: LOVE #83

Thursday, 20 August 2020

Through the underground dungeons
and the thick muddy jungle,
through the layers of onions
and vines that do strangle,

You seem to find pathways
that lead to solutions,
resourceful as always
to bring resolution.

This bouncing back matters.
You've found new support.
There will be no tatters,
instead, there's a fort.

With Love, I'll be filling
the garden and flowers.
I know you are willing
to develop your powers.

So onward we surf
across a new ocean.
We're into new turf.
The HeartMath's in motion.

FROM: LOVE #84

Friday, 21 August 2020

I felt your bigness and your power
in your meditation hour;
softly present without question
no use for any suggestion
for your YOU was very clear –
a big heart that I hold dear.

There's a fierceness slowly mounting
with these days that we've been counting.
Love is growing without measure.
Let us not forget the pleasure
so essential and inspiring
to the wholeness you're aspiring.

You have earned this golden crown
and the lion courage found.
To the quantum field we go,
Let's "sit back, enjoy the show"!

FROM: LOVE #85

Saturday, 22 August 2020

It's a brand-new day
for finding center
for opening windows
for bouncing back
for high vibrations
for looking good
for honing in
for spiraling up
for planting hopes
for LOVING YOU!

FROM: LOVE #86

Sunday, 23 August 2020

Expanding with you
brings me to higher ground.
Or is it that you are
expanding with me?
And you are finding yourself
on higher ground?
Is there a shift in the matrix?
Do I sense an opening?
a shedding?
What is it that has altered
your presence
that you feel so different?
Surely it's not just the
clean floors,
the trimmed hedges,

the weeded garden,
the ironed clothes,
the pedicured toes.
Maybe your immersion
in the world of Love
is inviting you in
to a new place.
Maybe the song is
taking hold.
Maybe Love really does
lift us up
where we belong.*

*This was not intentional, but the poem ended with this reference to Joe Cocker & Jennifer Warnes. "Up Where We Belong" from *An Officer and a Gentleman*, Stewart Levine, 1982. Movie soundtrack.

FROM: LOVE #87

Monday, 24 August 2020

In your natural opening
of the window to the outside
world, I see you
hearing new stories,
and hear you speaking
new insights.
I sense you sharing
from a different place
as you notice simultaneous
co-existence of the
inside with the out.
Your allies on the path
enrich your reflections
and highlight questions
that can only get bigger

answers through open
conversation.
Their own explorations
spark curiosity
and delve deeper into
what makes a person
want to change?
Pain, and frustration, anger
or sheer boredom of patterns
may send a spark,
but they will only ignite
the flame of change
when we embrace
the response-ability we have
for our own experience
our own perception,
our own life.
This is where the change starts.
At the center.
Right now, your center
is full of my Love for you,
and that deep desire
to align with your own truth.
The next step is to look through
the window and see where

we might go
from here.

FROM: LOVE #88

Tuesday, 25 August 2020

Ahoy, Sailor Lei, who played hooky this day.
Instead of your homework, you opted to play.
You followed your passion to be in the weather.
The winds were terrific for sailing together.

The conditions were perfect for stretching your
    learning;
your confidence growing with skills you were
    earning...
a creative solution for reefing the sail
brought forth a new insight, and lifted a veil.

Awareness of options in new situations
merged past with the present through
    imagination

Resourced by combining your skills and your
   knowledge.
You presenced yourself, and were willing to
   call it.

This learning with Love, of "Yes, I can do this"
built trust in the you who's got
   "figure-it-out-ness."
And then there's the docking, "outstanding,"
   he said.
Dreams of your own boat floating 'round in
   your head.

Hooray for the learning of learning you found.
It broadens potential for which you are bound.
So skipping your duties had its own rewards:
enhancing the future that you will go towards.

FROM: LOVE #89

Wednesday, 26 August 2020

Wrapped in today's Love
is a bouquet of joy.
Just like the snowdrops of Spring
are a sign that other flowers will follow,
this bouquet is a
tell-tale of a momentous
shift in your own seasons.
One that while inviting in
the new, is also
an unfolding of the original joy
you came here with.
You know this joy...
of freedom and security,
of confidence and play,
of connection and sovereignty,

of intuition and spirit.
Its depth wells up from
the crystalline core, and
radiates out into expressions
of color and shape and scent.
Basking in its fresh perfume,
you can touch into an imagination
and open to what had not
seemed possible
until now.

FROM: LOVE #90

Thursday, 27 August 2020

Each day you write
I get to discover
another way to say,
"I love you."
Through rhymes & images,
metaphors and flow,
the words of their own
accord align with
my unfolding Love
for you – fresh
as the garden tomatoes,
juicy as the peaches
ripened by the summer heat.

Each day is a surprise,
an original twist of fate
that emerges in the moment,
yet there is a steadiness
in the essence of our
coming together like
two rivers bound
for the same ocean.
And just like the swelling rivers
from the afternoon rains,
my Love grows more
abundant with
each day you write.

FROM: LOVE #91

Friday, 28 August 2020

They're over now,
the stories past,
and while the clarity
continues to bring you
reassurance of your sanity,
the exploration sometimes
hurts.
The pain is still stored
somewhere in hiding,
afraid to come out
for fear that its
expression will
make it all worse
again.
The sorrow of

ignorance
that didn't know
any better
feels heavy
as you realize now
that being powerless with
no protection wasn't meant
to be normal.
Now, so many "if only's"
surface to try to
alleviate the naked truth.
And though I too want
to soothe the cracks in
your wounded heart,
I want to pause first
and recognize
the anguish, the confusion,
the doubt and fear
that had you languish
in these traps of
obedience.
Then the guilt that
followed when you
sought your own voice,
and dared to speak.

In this pause, I hold you close
so you will know
I'm with you.
I see the stories
broken down,
the mechanics revealing
an imposed fake glory.
And as they lose their power,
you regain your
pure essence.
Hold my hand
so you can release
your grip on these
old stories.
They no longer serve you;
I do.

FROM: LOVE #92

Saturday, 29 August 2020

I love your inside scoop;
the dark green walls
of renewal welcoming in
energies of creativity.

I love riding the upward spiral
with you, pressing on
the upward way as a
melody would waft up into the air.

I love the tone of the field
you have set about generating,
to gather the pieces you once
lost along the way.

I love the extra flavors you
add to the expresso that give
your body extra powers,
enhancing its magical dark roast.

I love the free agents
who are forming a dynamic circle
of wisdom, spontaneity and
deep care for the world, including you.

I love being with your playful
self in laughter and giggles
at the clever humor you
share with funny friends.

I love your willingness
to experiment, to persist,
to reach out, to try, to feel,
to care, to forgive, to love.

I love you in your wholeness
even with the scars
and the hesitation at times,
your beingness evolving into congruence.

I love being with you –
the fullness of the life energy
winding its way through your day
with the hope that your deep
work will be of service to ALL.

FROM: LOVE #93

Sunday, 30 August 2020

By now you know you're not alone....
Patterns and phenomena in
systems of dysfunction
that others too have lived through
on one side,
and the solid company
of support on another.
Your developing discernment
allowing the pieces of the
puzzle to fall into the
semblance of an image,
some finding new places
to settle,
others falling off the table
altogether

and new ones surprising
you with the beauty
they bring to the picture
that, as it grows,
will need another table
to hold it for its
magnificence.
Even if there were no puzzle,
you know you're not alone now,
because underneath it all,
you know I am here.
You know I will be,
even if you don't write,
and as you stay connected
to me, the picture
will continue its
unfolding into
magnificence
even without the table
to hold it up.
For by then,
it will no longer
be an image,
it will be
your life.

FROM: LOVE #94

Lundi, 31 Août 2020

Juste une fois
pendant ces 100 journées
d'expression
je voudrais t'appeler
mon amour
ma chérie
mon chouchou
mon minou
ma lionne
mon désir
mon trésor
mon bijou
ma belle
ma bien-aimée...
T'avouer que je garde

tous mes bisous
amoureux pour toi
et te dire que
cette beauté pure
d'un cœur précieux
me réjouit l'esprit.
Je me sens bien
chez toi
et en ta présence
adorable.

FROM: LOVE #94 - Translation

Just once
during these 100 days
of expression
I would like to call you
my love
my dear
my darling
my kitty
my lioness
my desire
my treasure

my jewel
my beautiful
my beloved…
To confess that I keep
all my kisses
in love for you,
and tell you that
this pure beauty
of a precious heart
thrills me.
I feel good
with you
and in your adorable
presence.

FROM: LOVE #95

Tuesday, 1 September 2020

Oh, the fields you've crossed –
those windy roads of incertitude
weaving their way through
the tall grasses kept you
from seeing where you were
headed.
So instead, you went
off trail.
Honing in on the elements
bigger than your eyes
to help guide you and
see beyond where you were,
you turned inwards to your
newly calibrated compass, to
the wisdom of

your beating heart
and the music
flowing through your blood.
The darkness helps
you see more clearly
because you let go
of your eyes and move into
the realm of intuition,
where the plethora of
vision opens potential,
quenches the thirst
for wholeness,
and brings the
contentment of belonging.
It matters not there is no trail.
This is where you are happy.
I know this, since this is
where I find you again and again,
because this is where your heart opens,
and you remember me.

FROM: LOVE #96

Wednesday, 2 September 2020

Back to the Bay
that links the
ocean
and the moon
in its fullness
tonight...
the moon sends ripples
of joy as you
glimpse it intermittently
through the stormy
clouds offering
lightning and thunder
in all their splendor.
Rain drips into
your dinner party

to remind you
that it matters
where you sit.
Laughter rounds out
the sweet reminder of
innocent love crushes
from childhood,
and the stories
linger on in the night,
blessed by moonlight,
blessed by the star
at the top of the mast.

FROM: LOVE #97

Thursday, 3 September 2020

Sleep, Lavinia, Sleep.
I will watch the boat
for you
swinging on its anchor through
the night of rain
and thunder.
May you dream
in melted slumber
lightning was and
is no longer,
striking near
and getting stronger.
Calm is back
with gentle patter.
Darkness joins in

on the matter.
Space for rest
inside the cabin.
Time for dreams
of what may happen
on the morrow
with the sunshine
new-found winds
and loving of mine.
Eastward towards
the sun we'll sail.
Now you sleep,
let rest prevail.

FROM: LOVE #98

Friday, 4 September 2020

Today is blessed
with light and mild,
your sweet heart
still soft and wild.
I love you
with all my being,
playful funny
fully seeing
all your beauty
in and out
kindness too,
there is no doubt.
Friends in touch
from far & near.
They too love you,

it is clear.
May you rest
assured tonight
that our Love
will treat you right.
Coming with
respect and care
superpowers
depth and flair.
Nighty night,
it's time to sleep.
All this Love
is yours to keep.

FROM: LOVE #99

Saturday, 5 September 2020

The glimpse into the
outer world
gives practice
to your training

decision-making
with the weather
windy, sun
or raining

These skills are natural
from before,
what's new's the
opening shell.

The one you're
coming out of now
with me
to wish you well.

Hold steady
in the work you've done,
you're sailing
in new waters.

To be yourself
with company
for days,
amongst the yachters.

And so you did,
all through the day
keep listening
from inside.

There's no more
reason to hold back
and no more
need to hide.

Your presence
is a part of this.
We need you
for the balance.

The teamwork
of including all,
with Love-filled
strength and valiance

FROM: LOVE #100

Sunday, 6 September 2020

The outer marshmallow layer,
too soft and too sweet
that served to hide
the inner steel cage
bound around your heart,
and even burned itself
in the bonfires
of useless drama
to show it could take
anything,
has melted away now.
As your heart re-kindles
its desire to move
in flow, it takes
its first steps with

timid curiosity
through the open
cage door,
testing what it feels like
to stretch its wings.
There is a lingering
rigidity, that stems
from its frozen past,
that too will slowly melt
as you learn to trust
the genuine nature
of your Love from within.
One hundred poems
from me to you
have given you a sense
I come with Love
of many forms, and
will be with you hence.

EPILOGUE

So, what was the process like? At first, the tricky task of actually understanding what I was feeling was stifled by my own judgmental ear. Judgment dominated. Honesty was challenging. I felt shy. Love felt scary. I was guarded and hypervigilant – fear was a habit. But I kept going back to Don Miguel Ruiz's description of what Love was not, and I kept listening and opening, slowly, respectfully, for something else, until I found a space of radiant peace, of comfort, of reliable support, of unwavering compassion, intricate understanding and boundless care.

To listen from here, I had to slow way down and open to a spaciousness that held everything, inspired by a meditation style of Craig Hamilton's. It was only from *here* that I was able to transmute self-judgment into understanding, shame into integrity, fear into courage, and on it went... Sometimes it was only through writing from *this* space that I could figure out what I was feeling and what I actually needed. My frozen self could finally thaw out, come to life and fully feel. *This* is where I could feel the purity of all emotions. I noticed some emotions were easier for me to feel than others.

Over time, though difficult emotions still lingered, a lightness emerged, with a trust alongside it, and I developed a comfort in the midst of discomfort. My capacity to honor, and to be with 'what is' expanded. It was through this experiment that I developed a discernment between the voices in my head. And with determination, I found the reliable truth that no matter what I was feeling, I could always access Love, even if sometimes it took longer to find that connection. Love always had something to tell me.

Whether it was to feel enveloped in the softness of a loving hug, to acknowledge what I had been through with compassion, to witness either the feelings themselves or what it took to move through them, to presence a truth I didn't want to see, or whether it was to connect different feelings into one insight, to unwrap a completely unexpected lesson, to further develop a wisdom I had tapped into, to nudge me into action, or just to express a desire to enjoy the moment or even to play, the diverse responses I received every day were fresh and always relevant.

In these conversations with Love, I felt seen, heard, valued, respected, known. I found Love to be generous, attentive, wise, fair, available, kind, honest, willing, present, reliable. It was never domineering, manipulative, deceitful, harmful. Love felt like a friend, a guide, an ally, worthy of trust. Just by how Love spoke to me, I was inspired to show up more fully as myself, my best self. Love gave me courage. Love liked to celebrate.

In the end, I learned that when I was in the energy of Love, I made better decisions. I communicated more gracefully. I could listen more openly. I was a better friend. I trusted myself more. I was more confident. I was sovereign. I felt precious and beautiful and strong. I was more relaxed. I had nothing to prove, nor did I seek approval. I could hold space for others; I could better see their greatness and their struggles. I felt more gratitude. I was authentic. I had more compassion for myself and others. I was worthy. I was free, as were others. I was no longer grasping, no longer seeking validation, no longer defensive, no longer insecure.

What if everyone accessed this? What if everyone could feel truly deeply connected to Love. I bet domestic violence would drop. I bet systemic fear would drop. I bet systemic racism wouldn't carry such a heavy hook to those who feel threatened by its demolishment, and people would be more inclined to be inclusive, more able to hold space for each other, more able to listen with compassion. Clearly this is not a comprehensive solution to systemic fear, racism, or narcism. But it could be solid foundation from which to initiate change.

What did I learn about Love? It is the most powerful force of life. It is the only energy that can hold absolutely any kind of emotion, or experience, with grace. It is the alchemical force that turns fear, guilt, shame, insecurity, anger, confusion, and any other emotion, including joy, into pure energy, authenticity and humility. It aligns with dignity and integrity for all. It supports discernment between what expands your quality of life, and what contracts it. It supports decision-making aligned with your pure essence. It simplifies your ability to sense who and what resonates with your true self, that beautiful bad-ass that you are. It is replenishing. It allows you to feel full, so that when you come into relationship with another, instead of coming from a place of lack or fear, you can arrive whole-hearted, and with a big smile, knowing that you will be loved and cared for, no matter what. Your own connection to Love, always accessible, provides ample support, care, and guidance. And best of all, it's abundant; available to all, anywhere, anytime, in your own inner landscape.

After I stopped, I missed it so much, I committed to another 100 days… so I have now written over 200 poems from Love. That second round may come out later…

BIBLIOGRAPHY

Just Mercy. Directed by Destin Daniel Cretton, Warner Bros. Pictures, 2019

Lewis, John and Michael D'Orso. *Walking with the Wind: A Memoir of the Movement*. New York: Simon & Schuster, 1998. Print.

Ruiz, Miguel Angel, M.D. and Janet Mills. *The Voice of Knowledge: A Practical Guide To Inner Peace*. San Rafael: Amber-Allen, 2004. Print.

Whyte, David. *Just Beyond Yourself: the Poetry of Robust Vulnerability*. Langley: Many Rivers, 2020. Online Zoom series - 3 Sundays in May.

www.ingramcontent.com/pod-product-compliance
Lightning Source LLC
Chambersburg PA
CBHW022050290426
44109CB00014B/1044